Cooking with Cancer

Julian Flanagan

COOKING WITH CANCER

Cooking with Cancer
published in the United Kingdom in 2017
by Leslie Bell trading as Mica Press
47 Belle Vue Road, Wivenhoe, Colchester, Essex CO7 9LD

www.micapress.co.uk | books@micapress.co.uk

ISBN 978-1-869848-17-0

Cover design by Les Bell and Shannon Griffiths
with
photography © Eleanor Flanagan 2017

Preface

This collection is my wife's fault. Her adherence to that awkward "in sickness" clause, and her notable all round brilliance, made me capable of writing it. As did our delightful children's cheery, unfussy understanding. My wider family of Flanagans, Gibbons and VJs gave, as always, ever-present sustenance, so too my enduring, lively tribe of friends.

The Royal Marsden Hospital, Chelsea, is an almost miraculous place, the people who work there, receptionists to surgeons to cleaners to assistants, remarkable. There I was lucky enough to be treated by Professor Tekkis, Mr Rasheed and their expert colorectal gang; Professor Cunningham's gentle, attentive chemotherapy crew; radiotherapists and phlebotomists, technicians and consultants who ease the wary through intimidating scanners and the most embarrassing of procedures. Dr Richard Towers of the Psychological Support Department helped keep me sane. The jovial stoma nurses of the Chelsea and Westminster Hospital made the weird acceptable.

And day after day, on wards, in treatment rooms and day units, the Marsden's nurses acted with a kindness, consideration and devotion to their role that is sometimes hard to explain.

My deepest gratitude goes to them and to everyone who has helped me.

Acknowledgements

"Afterwards you might feel a tingling when you touch something cold" first appeared in *Lighthouse,* Winter 2017.

'One Night's Stay' first appeared in *The Reader,* issue 67, September 2017.

To Frances, my patient lifeline,
and Megan, Charlotte, James.

Starters

Main Course

Afters

Digestif

Starters

An English Patient

On the parade to diagnosis,
turning through hooped scanners
and narrowing possibilities,
one idiot hope tagged along:
that I did have cancer,
that it was blood in the bowl
because if, after all the fuss,
it was only the beetroot I'd been eating,
the embarrassment could kill me.

Two creases cup the registrar's smile,
brackets downplaying the joke.

Frances is holding my hand.

As if confiding a recipe,
he explains the cancer loaded in my colon
and cocked to scatter through me.

Our pressed lifelines double back:
Parents – Honeymooners – Teenagers
London – Venice – Preston.

His chubby mouth fixes a grid across the seasons.

Her criss-crossed palm is a net catching fear.

"Radiotherapy this summer....
....chemotherapy pills..."

Love dodges
the registrar and fluorescent light.

"...remove the tumour in autumn...
....stoma bag for a year...."

It scatters to Megan, Charlotte and James
ignorant in their classrooms.

"...winter and spring chemotherapy...
...infusions this time..."

Who will pack up and return
to home's cordon sanitaire

"...stoma bag removed autumn next year"

and be infected by this truth.

Half a detached day
into this motif of cancer
I kiss Frances on the ENO's steps.
St. Martin's Lane rolls with freed workers,
West End promise and now family,
wine-swept from supper
waving down the Friday night pavement.
Bugger cancer, we'll hide in opera.

And when the spotlight corners an aria
and galleries tip around the baritone,
the sinew of his voice
replaces word meaning,
works thoughts loose:

twin family snapshots
wash up in my head, bleed together;
a Trough of Bowland stream and Rub al Khali sand
soaking our day-tripping feet with the same liquid shock
40 years apart
and the tumour slips away
as parents become children, nieces turn into aunties
in sand fells and moss dunes.

ONE NIGHT'S STAY

My hotel room is in the eaves.
A plastic kettle shoulders the ceiling.
Blinds portion woodpigeoned air.
Over shuffling firs and the afternoon village
in rooms where he knows no one,
my eleven year old dyspraxic son
attempts a day's lessons, a night's boarding
in the hope next year this school
will want to find the pattern
under the debris of his attention.

My mobile suckles reception
at the open window.
As I wait, hoping they don't call,
the eaves become the hollow bush
where we'd scoop mud for treasure
with his Bob The Builder digger;
become last Friday's scanner
booming a call like wild cranes
as its magnets mined my cancer's limits;
become two praying hands
cupped above his fears.

MEDICINAL

Terracotta platoons
empty from their foil sentry boxes,
lead off into my interior.
In working week slots
radiotherapy's light-thread and calculation
floss the tumour.

It becomes a distillery of assorted loves –
cards, hugs, emails,
a carpet bombing of Hail Marys –
a surprise cocktail pressed on me,
soul-spinning,
clear as moonshine.

.

THERAPISTS

The room wobbles on the cusp of humiliation:
kneel on the palette, trousers round your knees
(bladder full, as requested)
lie forward, pull your boxers down.

But before you slide under the machine
and its beam drills your geology
of fat, muscle and bone,
the radiotherapists adjust your hips,
flanks, just slightly, with young hands,
the touch of settling a baby in a cot

and all the time they talk,
remembering things you said
about your life outside this room,
lopping shame with a scalpel of chat,
wielding it to insist
you are more than a serving of embarrassed flesh.

Bad Language

The stoma looks tolerable,
a pricked nub of intestine
nosing from skin, cherry-neat
in passive brochure black and white.

It's the captions about the stoma bag
that unsettle:
"velcro ears" "adhesive flange"
"leakage crease".

Four of us wait for the radiotherapy hulk
to turn its eye.
Equal as a confessional queue,
we recite the penance for treatment:
swollen minutes buried in the MRI scanner,
infused hours, soured days.

Then the youngest leans into the space
where our voices meet.
Tired? Stay in bed, long as you like.
A good day? Do a favourite thing.
Think forward to when it will be over.

And he talks about Jamaica,
treasure island crosses
already plotted on his calendar,
his brother's house "up country",
where he can measure time
by the drowsy hill climb of a Super Star bus,
air's slow loosening after thunder.
Or, not measure it at all.

ON MY SIDE

The surgeon is behind me,
on a recce, the only time
he doesn't look me in the eye.

The soft-voiced Filipina nurse
encourages my knees up the couch,
her small hand on my shoulder.

The surgeon's finger rummages.
"I'm just going to insert a small telescope."
Small like Jodrell Bank.

The Royal Marsden Chapel

Even when I nip in, kneel, and out,
the chapel's Victorian sidestep
from a corridor of 21st Century nerves and typefaces
is a weighted exhalation.
Behind the back wall's stained glass
are million pound scanners, ipoded patients.

But this don't-mind-me Anglicanism persists
in herds of hassocks,
still-polished plaques to founders,
the baize board feathered with post-it-notes,
a sticky plantation of prayer
offered up on the altar every Thursday.

The one thing missing
is a figure on the altar's empty cross
trying to lever himself up to breathe,
who doesn't offer me an explanation,
or an excuse, but recognition,
skin-tasselled, nailed-down, recognition.

COOKING WITH CANCER

Taste buds skewed by chemotherapy,
I scrabble for something to eat –
microwaved mozzarella with anchovies,
frankfurters dripping guacamole,
a palm of Skittles, a bite of Cheshire,
an Uncle Joe's Mint Ball from the stately, 1.4kg jar.

The mints haunt my pockets and corners of rucksacks,
maroon totems, plucky charms,
tribal medicine: Leigh, Lancashire, 1915,
where the trees on Beech Walk
are carved with soot and lovers' initials
and Uncle Joe's sell by the ounce in Market Place.

At gates emptying ancestors,
a 15-year-old miner and 15-year-old mill girl
who will smuggle kindness like a holy relic
through the century,
come from stained air
to thin margins of freedom.

And race against them on cinder,
Pop running the mile, Nana the dash.
Balloon them with their voices,
twisting Latin masses from the choir loft
to loop St. Joseph's ash-thin pillars;
gilding the church hall with light opera.

Pop was still unfurling his tenor in his seventies,
The Desert Song in their scrubbed Eccles flat,
laughing at a maddened grandson
trying to hear the telly, who did not recognize
a serenade to hunger,
to the demands we should make on life.

My hand scrambles in the jar,
plucks a cellophane-wrapped taste
of that cane sugar sweetness,
oil of peppermint, cream of tartar, strength.

HOLD ON A MINUTE

Charlotte's milk cup would flop aside,
her breaths slow in the cot.
My hand would slide from her dimpled fist.
Then she'd grab back, whimper,
my cigarette and wine delayed.

Frances lets me sleep in,
fattening me for the carve up.
When I make the kitchen it's empty,
Megan and Charlotte tube-rattling to school.
Half awake I text, grabbing them back.

James and I look down from the back row.
Lightstrips edge the steps and aisles.
Again I am looking down through
that Airbus night window at post war Baghdad,
its street web, black geometry and silence.

"I want the loo Dad. It's alright, I'll go by myself."
James takes the steep flight sideways,
foot by calculated foot,
down towards absence,
boarding school's invasion of his life.

Late Prom at the Albert Hall

Frances and I look up from a *tranquillo* crowd
at figures tiny as crotchets flecked in the Gallery

like the figures in *A Matter of Life and Death*
at skylights above heaven's library of souls

before Abraham Sofaer as the film's celestial judge,
and brooding surgeon, passes sentence.

Main Course

The Beginning of Treatment

We leave James tethered to the promise
of a first night barbecue
and weekends at home,
his new school shirt still creased
by the cardboard's hug.

We lay the table one place short
and are followed into every room
by an empty plot of air,
a poltergeist that leaves furniture untouched
and upturns everything.

Pre-Op Assessment

Our Lady of Dolours, Fulham Road,
never feels Chelsea-Catholic.
The painted Victorian stations and cranny saints
surprising you with wounds and smiles
are like the old Warrington churches
we'd shuffle into late on 70s Sundays,
their congregations refugee echoes
of Famine and Reformation.

There are Anglo-Irish here too,
their council blocks tipped at the river,
the estate at the World's End,
and Portuguese, Poles, Filipinos.

So I don't know what accent
will sift through the confessional grille
when I kneel and attempt
a surgical wipe of my soul.

The tongue is London;
its words bite,
"Do understand when I say
love is not a feeling, it is a decision,
and you must be generous with it,
giving it patiently and giving time".
Even if your time is unknown.
Which means everyone.

HIDE AND SEEK IN THE DARK

The children run flaunting torches
down the trough of garden,
under their city's bloodied-swab clouds.
The buildings are negatives of day,
light from their giant dolls' house windows
partying the grass.

Will the operation be like this equipoise
of beauty, puzzle and fear?
Or like later, inside,
James chattering about Minecraft,
digging out diamonds, iron, elusive rubies
then looking from his dark tablet –
"I've fallen down my coalmine".

The Night Before

A beck of glucose dips into my arm.
An oxygen pump mutters at the next bed.

The surgeon had come, jacket on, almost home,
genially laid out my intestines with a pencil,
apologised for his drawing
(bad with his hands?)
showed me what they would do,
what could go wrong,
gave fear a manageable percentage
to lodge beside trust and luck.

The hospital flickers on,
the city's night light.

Scurrying to service the laxative,
insistent as a Carry On gag,
I spot Cafe Roma over the road,
the familiar, red crayony sign,
the memory of its signed Roma shirts
and terraced ciabattas behind glass,
the reassuring idea that it will be opened up
around the time I am.

A late bus tuts.
A streetlamp butters the ceiling with windows.

CHANGED

The loose gown and taut stockings
are like enlistment,
the fabric persuading you as it touches skin
of cutting,
coming soon.

I look up to the gentle anaesthetist,
haloed by ceiling light,
my trolley angled at the theatre door.
A voice, an idea of movement,
in there.

Awake.
Drugged light.
Asleep?
"This is the om, this is like consciousness, the different forms of it."

A new burgundy smock.
A new face.
Always someone keeping watch.
"The eye with the peacock, this is Krishna."

Time gutted of night, hours, certainty of sequence.
Awake.
Nurse Jai's tattooed arm, reaching across.
Asleep.

Night Ward

Sleep unlaces.

Night presents
as monochrome and sweat.
Gullivered in tubes I snatch morphine
with the Nite Life neon button
shisha-looped at the bedhead.

The nurses come unbidden every something hours.
A soft-footed law through the principalities of curtain,
they bend over bedside readings of heat and blood,
top up gills plumbed into my neck and back,
leave with "Good night" benedictions.

In a fracture of curtain,
Stan's restless face across the ward,
skin puttied by his Anglepoise.
Clive strides around in tight Y-fronts
hunting a chat.

I "sleep".

Nurse: "Hello sir, can you hear me? Excellent.
Can you open both your – excellent.
Can you squeeze my hand, hard as you can?
That's a bit girly. That's better."

Curtains scope around his folding life,
body shapes against them like a party marquee,
and the hurrying in and out,
hard breathing, of a wedding dance.

Stan: "He sounds like he's dying.
We're all people who are getting well in here.
He shouldn't be in here.
It's disgusting."

Solicitors bring a late offering of embarrassed questions,
ask if he's ever been married, had children.
Do you have brothers or sisters?
Do you own your home? Do you rent it?

Stan: "I shouldn't have said that,
last night, about him.
It wasn't right.
I just don't like being near death."

STAN, MONOLOGUE ARTIST

*"It all went wrong in the 60s when I found
a Dexedrine pill in my brother's pocket."*

A clown's nose of stoma pokes from my waist.

*"How did I come off heroin? Got methadone from my doctor.
Locked myself in for four and a half months."*

A jelly fish catheter hangs on my line.

*"The only person I can get on my phone is my wife.
And she won't talk to me."*

A ladder of staples climbs my stomach.

*"My Dad used to hit me. I never hit my kids.
But they hit theirs, slapping their legs."*

A morphine dragonfly feeds my hand.

*"I can't keep my mouth shut.
I've been punched in the face that many times and slapped by women.
I can't keep my mouth shut in front of anyone."*

INSIDE ALL THAT TIME

A nurse reaches across the curtain, closes night.
Outside, cold slumps on Cafe Roma's awning
and our old route to primary school.

As the children's weaving tread
made this stretch of Fulham Road
a building block in their shared memory

as their vignette passed this window,
Megan's beret tilted, Charlotte's always plum,
James in a tribe of buckled caps

as their doodle of rucksacks and hurry
barged into the background
for a decade's patients

the tumour grew

cap by blazer by shoe size
and was outgrown
by love's tangled metastasis.

Afters

Out in Glorious Technicolor

After the pared ward,
black, uncubicled sky
and colour:
streetlights bent over their yellow nights,
pubs dressed by Quality Street,
the traffic lights' fruit gums,
home's psychedelia of mugs, cushions, scarfs, bananas.

MASQUERADE

Someone is playing *Masquerade,*
an optimistic pollen of notes
chiming air
from piano to sitting room to corridor
and through a door
to where I kneel
squeezing the bag into the toilet bowl,
wiping its open mouth clean,
listening to *Masquerade*, choosing that.

AID FROM THE DEVELOPING WORLD

Lying on the kitchen sofa, I watch the ceiling
and talk to the Congolese nurse.
She examines the staple line running through
my navel's open cast mine –
swirls of red, black seams,
a bruised yellow river draining south.
Then pliers them out. Some hurt.

But she is from Congo, where Frankenstein platoons
build soldiers from the leftovers of children
and make children through the tip of a machete.
So we talk and sometimes I take
a deeper breath,
and say it's fine when she asks if it hurts
because she allows this to count as pain.

"AFTERWARDS YOU MIGHT FEEL A TINGLING
WHEN YOU TOUCH SOMETHING COLD"

Jacket off, home, the first infusion ticked,
I sow the flat with hedgerow life.
Thistles sprout in damp laundry.
Nettles stream from the tap.
A hedgehog balls in my mouth
on a spoon of milk and Frosties.

MEGAN

One earphone in, one abseiling her jumper,
a thicket of hopes under straightened hair,
she seems half away already, university-primed,
riot shield eyes deployed.

Then, mid-argument, she'll stop,
mumble her point back
or quell supper's skirmish of dishes for me,
worried I am chemoknackered.

And on her way out
to a friend, a film, a class,
she'll stop to hug, carefully on my left,
giving no platform to the bag.

SHOWING A LITTLE GRATITUDE

Half infused, I write Christmas cards
and remember with Nurse Maguire
the nicest times to smoke.
Plastic falling ivy
loops from wheeled stands,
awkward as skinny mannequins,
and drug sacks that float above our heads
like thought bubbles.

If we rose on our dizzy legs
took the mannequins' thin arms
and tried to roll their five splayed wheels,
we could treat them to a promenade,
rounding the sweets and puzzles trolley,
turning at the shelf of loyal paperbacks,
shambling nearly in time
to the suction pumps' wheeze and ping.

ROWER

Frances takes James to winter
grating skin with river air
at Craven Cottage.

I collect Charlotte, her face
clean tiredness
after rowing against the January tide.

We watch a fox cub
puzzling on its P.E.-sock paws
at the bank of the Fulham Palace Road

and a branch-wedged sunset;
buy hot chocolates from a dozing white café,
the cardboard warm against our palms,

against Charlotte's blisters,
swollen from pulling against the tide,
away from childhood.

Song Recital, 16 February, Wigmore Hall

Somehow the afternoon answers
these swamp weeks,
the suck of nausea
and leaks in the bag.

There is no hurry.
We wait under the cupola, its tableau:
a naked Soul of Music avoiding our eyes,
Harmony as light fracturing over Psyche and Love,
over our winter jackets and lost glasses,
Sunday papers and Oyster cards.

The baritone and pianist walk
from two oak doors, across a plain stage,
bringing only themselves,
registrars of air and wire,
consultants in the practise of stitching
Handel, Duparc and Mussorgsky
into us, threading them around us,
mending whatever needs it
with exact, blind precision.

CHEMONAUT

She dozes, a capsule of day room silence,
armchair tipped back for lift off.
Her scalp is cooled by a black cap,
wired like an Apollo astronaut's,
so her hair is not jettisoned
by the drugs as they spiral out,
claiming territory

catapult her on a mission –
mapped by appointment card
and a relay of nurses remembering her name –
whose destination is uncertain,
the hostility to life
in her colony of one, unknown.

The entryphone prises life open.
It's a home prescription,
administered at the kitchen table,
potent as gold top chemotherapy.

Initial effects are elation and tea.
Then ridicule, calmness, hysteria,
more tea, flashbacks:
the strap scalding our teenage palms;
night slug trails through the old Ealing flat;
that morning after, morning-suited stumble home.

Hugh arrives chortling, swinging his briefcase,
a weekly dosage.
Nick brings injections of hazy energy.
And Ben and Paul come, Sarah, Rupert and Vince,
discrete cures, turning up wanted but unasked
to what they could avoid,
braced for the delivery of themselves.

,

The waiting room tapers to a point,
one straight wall, one curved.
The shape describes its purpose:
a pause with flasks for tea and coffee,
biscuit packets transparent as our chemotherapy sacks.
A pause before the wine gum roll of a blood test
or we are cannulated next door for infusion
like a trolley of teapots.

But the shape is also possessive.
This space belongs to us
and our accessories to love
and we claim it
through couples greeting each other –
"Hello again!" "I'm still going!" –
their treatments attuned as astronomers
chasing phases of the moon;
we claim it
with a wife reading out a funny bit to her husband,
a daughter adjusting her mother's scarf,
a man brushing biscuit crumbs from his lover's lap.

More Bad Language

As I wibble with infusion before home
Nurse Wilson uses the full, confusing names
for my party bag of drugs.
I know them by their first names –
Metoc, Dexa, Carpo –
the Marx Brothers' less successful cousins.

Other cancer talk doesn't fit.
"Chemo" is too matey
"Victim" melodramatic
"Survivor" too Eastenders
and "Battling Cancer Dad"
too active, or comic –
a superhero Marvel dropped.

DRY

The kitchen makes do as the pub,
our mugs of tea do well as pints.

I nod to Bert, alert in the corner –
Charlotte's papier-mâché, art class mongrel.
"For a laugh I made a papier-mâché poo
and put it underneath. You know, out of paper."

"Ah, I see," says Ben. A beat.
"I thought you meant *you* had made it,
out of your bag."

In Good Company

The chemotherapy ends
and side effects wander off,
sway back like drunk guests,
amble away.

Some tiredness hangs around
and false memories of winter and summer –
numbed fingertips,
invisible sand caking my feet.

They are lessons in being James:
how blunted motor skills
make cabers of his pencils
and slide tackle his love of the beautiful game.

And the tiredness is a thin idea
of how it must be for him
aligning the world
with the orbit of his glitterball mind.

Digestif

"PATIENTS MAY BRING A BAG FOR THEIR BELONGINGS"

The red United rucksack
James took to boarding school
carries me into hospital.

The Ward of the Improbably Dressed

We can be found, say,
on a bed, mid afternoon,
in boxers and a glued-on bag.

Or wheeling a stand
like it's a nearly invisible friend,
the drip bag his empty face.

Or half-pyjamaed (either half)
with pipes in and out of any old orifice
or just one new one.

Visitors come bearing smiles,
cheeks chilled from those enormous streets,
exotic in full dress.

Unplugged

October seals the sky
at the screwed down sash
and I am debagged,
all of me back inside,
the bathroom a quickstep,
a light and dark shuttling
between the alkaline of nurses
and bowels signing off
a redundant, acid year.

Turret Room

Frances takes my hand.

She leads us from the ward
along the edge of a wing,
like a pier away from land.

I am clambered in clothes.
We wait for a take away of drugs
in the day room's chilly octagon.

Five windows suspend us,
a Rapunzel loop above buses'
red, riding hood roofs,

level with wind
tangled out from plane trees
and vaulting chimneys to the V&A,

the stone fingers
in its hollow tower
arched around peelings of sky

and permanently crossed.

Lightning Source UK Ltd.
Milton Keynes UK
UKHW021205200819
348272UK00009B/120/P